Haiku Nation

also by P.J. Reed

poetry

FLICKER

HAIKU NATION

HAIKU ICE

HAIKU YELLOW

HAIKU SUMMER

HAIKU GOLD

Haiku Nation

a collection of sizzling senryu and magical haiku
by P.J. REED

Lost Tower Publications

First published in 2017
second edition 2021
by Lost Tower Publications.
P.J. Reed asserts her copyright over this collection of her work.
P.J. Reed is hereby identified as the author of this work in accordance with Section 77 of the Copyright, Designs, and Patents Act 1988.
This book is sold subject to the condition that it shall not, by way of trade or otherwise, be lent, hired out or otherwise circulated without the publisher's prior consent in any form or cover than that in which it is published.

ISBN-13: 9781800498709 (IS)

Haiku Nation

P.J. Reed

Writer of Warlocks. Destroyer of Worlds.

Reed is an award-winning, multi-genre author with books ranging from high fantasy, horror, to haiku. She writes the Richard Radcliffe Paranormal Investigations series and the Bad Decisions series. Reed is also the editor and chief paranormal investigator for the Exmoor Noir newsletter.

She holds a BAEd from Canterbury Christ Church University, an MA from Bradford University and has dabbled in psychology with the OU.

Her writing has appeared in a wide variety of online and print magazines, anthologies, and collections.

In 2015, she was shortlisted for the National Poetry Anthology award. In 2018, P.J. won the Forward Press Poetry 'Circle of Life' competition for her poem 'The Empty Chair.'

In her poetry, Reed writes of the beauty and ethereal nature of the changing countryside in her series of haiku inspired collections, photographs, and poetry.

Reed lives in Devon, England with her two daughters, two rescue dogs, and one feral cat called Sammy.

For more information about Reed please visit one of the following websites:

Paranormal - https://pjreedwriting.wixsite.com/horror
Poetry - https://pjreedwriting.wixsite.com/poetry
Fantasy - https://pjreedwriting.wixsite.com/fantasy
Twitter - https://twitter.com/PJReed_author
Facebook - https://www.facebook.com/p.j.reedauthor

Introduction

The world of the poet seems an enchanted place. To stop, pause time and look deeply into the inner workings of the world is the fascinating concept which poets wrestle with every day. The depth of the artistic soul is laid bare in poetry. This creativity and sense of wonder is particularly found within the ancient form of Japanese poetry of haiku.

In traditional Japanese haiku the poem has three lines, where the first and last lines contain five *moras*, while the middle line has seven. The *mora* is a unit of sound in the Japanese language, which is similar to a syllable, but not the same. The *moras* cannot be translated into English and therefore syllables are used in their place. When westernised haiku is written as seventeen syllables divided into three lines of five, seven, and five syllables. Traditional haiku does not rhyme or contain punctuation but have a juxtaposition on the first or third line dividing the poem into contrasting parts. The haiku is usually written with natural and seasonal references with feelings and thoughts succinctly captured in one breathe.

Westernised haiku has developed as a poetry form straying somewhat from the tight constraints of its traditional Japanese masters but still contains that moment of beauty encapsulated in three small lines.

The poems in *Haiku Nation* offer an intoxicating insight into the ethereal world of haiku. The collection is divided into sections comprising: the Seasons, Mountains, Wanderings, and Waterfalling. The Seasons comprise of a sensitive exploration of the changes of nature throughout the year, found from P.J. Reed's long walks through the Devon countryside accompanied by her faithful companion, a rescued Jack Russell named Fizz. This series of poems reflect a deep investigation into the ways of nature and her poetry makes you look at nature with an altered perspective. The haiku 'see the warm rain drops,' is a dramatic, sensitive reinterpretation of a seemingly normal occurrence. While the poem, 'gunnera ripples' offers a beautiful image of the poet caught in a spring shower while walking.

The poet uses the concept of the seasons as a metaphor for the progress of people's life gently moving from the genteel progress of autumnal existence in 'elderly couples' to the fatality of winter and 'little grey cloud cries.' This concept is handled with great delicacy and beauty is found in all stages of life's journey.

The Wanderings section reflects this poet's love of travel with poems written on her travels throughout Europe and the Far East

The solitude of the poetic existence is also remarked upon in several haiku such as 'alone sea watching' when a beautiful moment is captured forever in words.

Haiku Nation is a breathtaking collection of powerful modern haiku which challenges the reader to seek out and see the world afresh.

by Karen Jones

Haiku Nation. Haiku World.

Haiku Nation Review

Simple, magical, real, imaginative, understandable. Also, brilliant and seen through the same eyes which the reader jointly shares. P.J. Reed's anthology, Haiku Nation, is a book of haiku poems. One of the simplest forms of poetry but hardest styles to write. The work here covers nature, emotions, and people. There are many memorable pieces in this volume's six themes (Spring, Summer, Autumn, Winter, Wanderings and Waterfalling). One example is the piece in the Winter section, it is overly powerful and dark.

> drowning with sorrow
> my tears would fill an ocean
> body why so frail

My first impressions are that the author, P.J., has been hurt immeasurably deeply by a love affair gone wrong. Placed in Winter, did it happen in winter, when the land is desolate, and the cold can kill you? Or is the poem about someone or something else? For example, a severe illness? There are poems that balance this out. For example, this joyous piece from the Waterfalling theme:

> orange sunset paints
> over sleeping blue waters
> Sun Moon lake, Nantou

This brings to mind a wonderful time spent at the Sun Moon Lake (in Taiwan). Simple but beautiful imagery straight from the heart. Almost a love poem, for a natural place and time enjoyed. My favourite poem is on page 23, in the Summer part. Being alone and almost in a dark mood is banished by a gift from the moon. Is this unconditional love and a love poem?

> I am loneliness
> the kind moon watches
> and sends me a shadow friend

The water colour art too adds to the character of the book. Many poetry collections are visually boring, being a mere 'book of words'; Haiku Nation is way more than just words.

Highly recommended for haiku poetry lovers and for readers in general. A very enjoyable and warm book. Even the dark pieces of work trigger strong emotions. A follow up volume would be most welcome. Spread the word, P.J. Reed is the haiku poet to read. A contemporary of Vannessa Daou.

by Nick Armbrister (Poet)

HAIKU NATION

Haiku Nation

Contents

First Line	Page
Biography	6
Introduction by Karen Jones	7-8
Haiku Nation Review by Nick Armbrister	10-11

Spring

a lone daffodil	20
bird songs after rain	21
confusion of feet	22
cool breezes whisper	23
earth salutes the sun	24
fuzzy black egglings	25
grey feather bundles	26
gunnera ripples	28
purple faces peer	29
softly cooing songs	30
spring wind lies sleeping	31
sun rises slowly	32
the dandelion	33
the ducks have landed	34
the old frosted pond	35

Summer

cloverfield parties	38
cooling shadows cross	39
dove deliveries	40
fluffy black stockings	41
hidden in the reeds	42
I am loneliness	43
intoxicating	45

memory of doves	46
natures' treasures smile	47
petal shards flutter	48
ruffled lily pads	49
sly eastern winds blow	50
the august sorrows	51
thinking of shared pasts	52
translucent wings	53

Autumn

a branchfull of leaves	56
a leaf floats slowly	57
distorted shadows	58
dragonfly flutters	59
drying rushes sway	60
elderly couples	61
forgotten grey path	62
green sycamore leaf	63
I am just a cloud	64
loneliness of one	65
oak branches shiver	67
oak tree is raining	68
rustles in silence	69
tired flowers sleep	70
touched by amber winds	71

Winter

a cold sun hangs low	74
bare branches no more	75
drowning with sorrow	76
grass-filled hollowings	77
hair whitens skin pales	78
hungry white-tailed dove	79
icy leaves stiffen	80
little grey cloud cries	81

my little cloud weeps	82
nighttime once more and	83
the fields are hidden	84
trees in negative	85
what is misery	86
winter storms arrive	87
wood pigeon towers	88
Wanderings	
cicada chorus	91
concrete boulders	92
fragrant cherry blossom	93
music pounds the beach	94
on ponds still water	95
orange sunset paints	96
red-faced walruses	97
shopkeeper perches	98
the earth is waking	99
the wind calls softly	100
the yellow moon hides	101
unrequited love	102
warm rain drops gently	103
whispered frosted breath	104
yellow sunflower paintings	105
Waterfalling	
alone sea watching	108
dart banded fish	109
flavours of the sea	110
gentle white waters	111
little rainclouds spill	112
little raindrops hide	113
orange sunset paints	114
raindrops are captured	115
rolling on the beach	116

Salcombe sands Devon	117
sculptures of the sea	118
shadowy grey leaves	119
the moon has fallen	120
the playful sea waves	121
the white water comes	122
yellow sails billow	123

Spring

The first touches of spring.

a lone daffodil
waiting by a muddied lane
first touches of spring

bird songs after rain
a chorus of happiness
the wood is perfumed

confusion of feet
bird steps scratched into the snow
travel in circles

cool breezes whisper
softly to the sleeping earth
dandelion yawns

earth salutes the sun
the yellowness of springtime
painted on the green

fuzzy black egglings
yellow beaks beep hungrily
moorhen nursery

grey feather bundles
sleeping on the riverbank
the white guard circles

HAIKU NATION

gunnera ripples
giant leaves our umbrellas
caught by springs showers

purple faces peer
shyly through the swaying grass
the gentle breeze smiles

softly cooing songs
gentle pairs of preening doves
I am only one

spring wind lies sleeping
birdsongs ring through the stillness
the hedge is tweeting

sun rises slowly
wind whispers spring is coming
to the melting earth

the dandelion
crowned white with wisdom bowing
grasses whisper praise

the ducks have landed
a ruffled V-shaped splashdown
tree reflections ripple

the old frosted pond
a careless frog jumps and plops
onto the frozen ice

Summer

The sweet scent of summer.

cloverfield parties
baseline buzz of flower nods
bumblebee banquet

cooling shadows cross
hot glare of a summer's noon
drooping flowers smile

dove deliveries
a path of frilled red poppies
suddenly appear

fluffy black stockings
sparkle with sprinkles of gold
carry lunch to go

hidden in the reeds
moorhen stands on lily pad
beeping as I pass

I am loneliness
the kind moon watches
and sends me a shadow friend

intoxicating
sweet scents of summery fruits
loiter in the air

memory of doves
grey feather fluffed with white
lying on the grass

natures' treasures smile
hidden by the swaying green
beauty is priceless

petal shards flutter
in a blossomfall of beauty
pinkification

ruffled lily pads
float on the greening river
yellow flowers burst

sly eastern winds blow
through the wavering grasses
betrayed by whispers

the august sorrows
crumbling cream rose petals fall
stolen by the breeze

thinking of shared pasts
apple blossom friends float past
on the summer breeze

translucent wings
black veined and improbable
pollenate the world

Autumn

The gold of autumn.

a branchfull of leaves
rush over lurking brown rocks
trees stand reflected

a leaf floats slowly
wandering with the river
autumn adventures

distorted shadows
circles of clouds reflected
ripple and vanish

dragonfly flutters
wings of finest cobweb silk
seen we walk away

drying rushes sway
brown velvet tops exploding
in a puff of seeds

elderly couples
sipping tea in symmetry
love is reflected

forgotten grey path
clothed in golden autumn leaves
moments of beauty

green sycamore leaf
hidden under running rain
I must walk with care

I am just a cloud
tossed by fickle autumn winds
leaf filled my path hides

loneliness of one
solitary leaf hanging
on an empty branch

oak branches shiver
in playful October winds
cold the old earth sleeps

oak tree is raining
flaming leaves twist and fall
squirrel sits beneath

rustles in silence
gentle plops of falling chestnuts
the river ripples

touched by amber winds
leaves dance in golden spirals
the white frost glistens

tired flowers sleep
red berries on the holly
welcome flocks return

Winter

The season of frozen beauty.

a cold sun hangs low
shadows stretch across the path
trees are white with mist

bare branches no more
hedges drip with feathered moss
fluffy winter coats

drowning with sorrow
my tears would fill an ocean
body why so frail

grass-filled hollowings
cobwebbed by an ice kissed dew
hidden from the sun

hair whitens skin pales
and I slowly fade away
as the oak regreens

hungry white-tailed dove
watches me and shares my lunch
people scurry by

icy leaves stiffen
glisten under moonlit night
fringed in frosted lace

little grey cloud cries
flowers fold their face away
so winter is mourned

my little cloud weeps
raindrops for my eulogy
too soon cries the wind

nighttime once more and
lonely moon asks for a friend
my bed lies empty

the fields are hidden
curious clouds bent too low
falling from the sky

trees in negative
wobble under river waves
waiting to regreen

what is misery
a soul that soars through mountains
tethered to a stone

winter storms arrive
in breathes of frozen beauty
the earth hides once more

wood pigeon towers
multifloored living space
eight birds to one oak

Wanderings

To explore and grow.

cicada chorus
cuts through heating morning air
palm trees are dancing

concrete boulders
infused with cigarette butts
blackened sea retreats

fragrant cherry blossom falls
pink clouds of perfume
startled sparrow sings and flies

HAIKU NATION

music pounds the beach
cars rumble and people scream
seagulls cry unheard

on ponds still water
falling raindrops draw circles
tree frog sits and croaks

orange sunset paints
over blue sleeping waters
Sun Moon lake, Nantou

red-faced walruses
big bellied and well basted
cooking in the sun

shopkeeper perches
squeezed into a plastic chair
guiltily we pass

the earth is waking
pathway crumbling underfoot
as ground leaps and groans

the wind calls softly
as insects hum in rhythm
natural harmonies

the yellow moon hides
veiled in red the mountain sleeps
under turquoise sky

unrequited love
climbers follow mountains call
bowing to the wind

warm rain drops gently
from dancing bamboo leaves while
the green snake shelters

whispered frosted breath
wrapped tightly in cloak of clouds
cold mountain shivers

yellow sunflower paintings
scattered on green fields
Okayama industries

HAIKU NATION

Waterfalling

The treasures of the sea.

alone sea watching
white waves sweep in and leave a
shiny pebble gift

dark banded fish dart
then bunch and scatter hiding
under clear blue sky

flavours of the sea
the tase of melted ice cream
on salt crusted lips

gentle white waters
softly tumble to the shore
shining pebbles bathe

little raincloud spills
bamboo sways and softly chimes
In warm waterfall

little raindrops hide
in an empty cloudless sky
thirsty pigeon waits

orange sunset paints
over sleeping blue waters
Sun Moon lake, Nantou

raindrops are captured
fall into ponds within ponds
as leaf overfills

rolling on the beach
sadness comes like greying waves
the sea wolf arrives

Salcombe sands Devon
paddle boats and sleepy yachts
lounging in the bay

sculptures of the sea
waves carve pictures on wet sand
in seaweed and shell

shadowy grey leaves
sailing on gold-tinged ripples
over rivers bed

the moon has fallen
lost below the rolling waves
sprinkled with star dust

the playful sea waves
and tugs at the drying sand
the shingle dances

the white water comes
thunder hidden in its waves
little fish have gone

yellow sails billow
as waving oceans tumble
sea murmurs secrets

The History of Haiku

Haiku is an ancient Japanese artform dating which originated from the Heian period of Japanese culture (700-1100). In this period, it was a requirement of polite society to be able to recognize, recite, and participate in *renga* or collaborative, long poetry writing activities at social events and lavish house parties. *Renga* was one of the most important literary arts in pre-modern Japan. The verses used sound unit counts of five-seven-five and seven-seven and finished with two lines of seven sound units each. At this time, poets considered the use of *utakotoba* as the essence of creating a perfect *waka* and use of any other words were considered unbecoming of true poetry.

A *hokku* was the opening stanza of *renga*. It had a special status in the poem and was written by the host or a guest of honour. A *hokku* was composed of seventeen moras or sound units broken into phrases of five, seven and five sound units respectively. Alone among the verses of a poem, the hokku included a *kireji* or cutting-word which appears at the end of one of its three phrases. Like all Japanese writing it was written vertically down the page and not horizontally as in western writing.

In the sixteenth century, with ongoing military conflicts within Japan and the eventual rise of the Tokugawa shogunate, Japanese poetry underwent a mini revolution becoming freer and less complicated.

By the time of the great *haiku* master Matsuo Bashō (1644–1694), the *hokku* had begun to appear as an independent poem and was also incorporated in *haibun* (a combination of prose and *hokku*), and *haiga* (combining a picture with a *hokku*). In the late 19th century, Masaoka Shiki (1867–1902) renamed the individual *hokku* poem *haiku*.

A traditional *haiku* poem has three lines, where the first and last lines contain five moras, while the middle line has seven. The *mora* is a unit of sound in the Japanese language, which is the Japanese equivalent to a syllable, but it is not the same. *Moras* cannot be translated into English and therefore syllables are used in their place. When westernized, *haiku* is written as seventeen syllables divided into three lines of five, seven, and five syllables.

Traditional *haiku* does not have a title, rhyme, or contain punctuation but they have a juxtaposition on the first or third line dividing the poem into contrasting parts. The *haiku* is usually written with natural and seasonal references with feelings and thoughts succinctly captured in one breath.

Glossary of Terms

Haibun	A combination of prose and haiku.
Haiga	A picture combined with haiku.
Haijin	The writer of haiku.
Haiku	Haiku is a highly structured form of Japanese poetry. In western culture haiku is easily recognisable from micro-poetry by its structure. Haiku is made of three lines. The first line contains five syllables, the second seven syllables and the third five syllables. Traditional haiku must contain certain elements such as a *kigo* and a seasonal element. It consists of a moment in nature captured and recorded.
Haiku Moment	The intense focus on one moment in time. To capture and freeze that image in haiku before it is lost or altered by the passage of time.
Hokku	The original form of haiku. The opening stanza to a *renga*. A long poem written by many people as a form of entertainment for the ruling elite of Japanese society.
Juxtaposition	When sentences are placed together with a contrasting effect.

Kigo	A word that implies the season of the haiku.
Kireji	A cutting word that denotes a break between the two parts of the haiku when writing in one-line Japanese poetry. There is no English equivalent to this although some poets may put a dash in their haiku to denote the change.
Koan	A *koan* is a Zen Buddhist contemplative phrase which contains a logical contradiction or paradox, designed to challenge the reader.
Mora	The *mora* is a unit of sound in the Japanese language, which is like a syllable, but not the same.
Sabi	The innate loneliness of life.
Senryu	A form of human haiku, expressing emotions or human actions. It has the same structure as haiku but does not have to contain a cutting word.
Syllable	A syllable is a single, sound unit of a word.
Tanka	A *tanka* is similar to haiku but consists of five lines and thirty-one syllables. Each line has a set number of syllables see below

Line one – five syllables

	Line two – seven syllables
	Line three – five syllables
	Line four – seven syllables
	Line five – seven syllables
Utakotoba	Words suitable to be used in songs or poetry.
Wabi	The austere and severe beauty of nature expressed through writings of spiritual solitude.
Waka	Traditional Japanese poetry.

How To Write Haiku

Everyone has their own writing style, and it is always important to let your writer's voice come through into your writing. However, some poetry is defined and recognisable by its external structure such as two-line Erdo love poetry, which as its name suggests has to contain two lines. Similarly, a sonnet is easily recognisable for consisting of fourteen lines written in iambic pentameter, while a limerick consists of five lines, written in a predominantly anapestic meter and have a strict rhyme scheme of AABBA. Likewise, traditional haiku has its own distinctly recognisable structure of three short lines. The first line contains five syllables, the second has seven syllables, and the last line consists of five syllables.

In the beginning, it is hard to contain your writing and thoughts within the narrow confines of haiku.
I tend to think of haiku writing as playing a game of chess. It requires practice, strategy, and mathematical precision. As with any skill, haiku thought needs hours of practise to attain, but with practice you will develop a way of thinking that automatically responds to the five-seven-five syllable scheme, which is immediately recognizable throughout the world as haiku.

I find my best haiku writing moments are away from people just walking with my dog, or alone and watching nature without the hindrance of man. I have been asked by several passers-by what I was doing, as I stood and memorized the mechanics of a droplet of water falling off a leaf. One man even stopped his car in a lane to find out the reason behind my unusual behaviour. In these situations, it is always better to reply that you are writing haiku and not in fact watching a leaf. One response will get such replies as 'very noble' and 'how exciting,' the other will get you a sideways glance and a wide berth.

Once I have observed an event and the tingling of a haiku begins to form, I try to write it down as soon as possible. Normally, when I write a haiku, the picture or memory is written within the first two lines of the haiku. The juxtaposition comes in the final line and will be either a comment on the picture formed, an extension of the image to other areas, or even what happened afterwards. For example, what happened to the leaf or droplet of rain after it had fallen. So, while the last line is still related to the first two it is obviously different.

Sometimes, when trying to write a haiku, it will not conform to the correct structure. However, a haiku should never be forced. It should be a natural extension of a scene. If the poem you are writing is either too big or too small to fit into the exacting haiku structure just accept that it is not going to be a haiku and write a poem or micro-poem instead.

Finally, the most important part of writing haiku is to have fun and not take it all too seriously.

Bibliography

"The Serious Side of Senryu," Edited by Alan Pizzarelli, Simply Haiku: A Quarterly Journal of Japanese Short Form Poetry. Autumn 2006, vol 4 no 3

"Senryu | Japanese Poem," Encyclopaedia Britannica. N.p., 2016. Web. 27 Dec. 2016.

"Senryu: Refreshing The Human Spirit". Haiku North America. N.p., 2016. Web. 27 Dec. 2016.

"Simply Haiku: Quarterly Journal of Japanese Short Form Poetry – Showcase," Simplyhaiku.com. N.p., 2016. Web. 27 Dec. 2016.

"Some Senryu About Go," Kiseido.com. N.p., 2016. Web. 27 Dec. 2016.

An Interview with P.J. Reed

Do you remember writing your first words of poetry?

My writing journey has been quite an interesting one. At school, the teachers could not understand why my writing was so slow, disordered, and generally just a little off. So, I kept my creative writing very private, creating my own stories on folded pieces of paper.

My writing career really began at university, by that stage I had learnt the skills to cope with creative writing and I was finally diagnosed with global dyslexia. However, my writing confidence massively increased when doing a poetry course and being told by the lecturer that I should take up a career in poetry. This was the first time anyone had encouraged me to do creative writing and it changed the course of my life.

My first poems were heavily influenced by my reading of the romantic poets as I had yet to find my own writing style. Some were still jumbled by dyslexia but the more I wrote the more coping skills I developed and after a few years I began to focus on writing short, narrative poetry.

My journey into haiku, which is probably the type of poetry I am best known for, started quite by chance over a decade ago. I was reading the poems in a LinkedIn group and I read this intriguing short form of poetry about nature. It was succinct and beautiful, like a picture painted with words. I embarked on a haiku odyssey learning about its origins in sixteenth century Japan, the distinct rules for writing authentic haiku, and reading the works of its greatest masters such as Basho. Finally, the teaching of haiku has come full circle and I give talks on the writing of haiku.

Does your background influence your writing?

I grew up in Bromley, Kent and had little knowledge of poetry. As I child I had a rhyming poetry book which I memorised. It was only after I moved to Devon and met previously unknown relatives that I realised writing poetry was part of my family history. One of my coal mining relatives used to write poetry in the 1950's in the back of an old blue school exercise book. It was lovely to discover that link. This move to Devon and my rediscovered heritage had a profound impact on my poetry. Much of the poetry I now write is based on experiences and observations of Devon nature.

What subjects inspire you to write?

The Devon countryside inspires much of my haiku poetry. However, my senryu is inspired by poetry by the people I see in their natural settings such as talking in cafes or on holiday. Whereas my haiku and senryu writing come from observations, the dark side of my poetry comes from an active imagination and the idea of 'What would happen if...?'

My writing process is quite simple. I write what comes into my thoughts. I think poetry should be a natural flow of words, so initially my poems are written on my phone, on receipts or anything I can access at a moment's notice when the inspiration arrives. Then later I try to decipher what I wrote as I copy them down into my 'official' poetry notebook.

Do you remember your first ever published work?

My first published poem was a long time ago. It was to be honest a terrible poem about lost love published in a collection of love poems by one of those publishers who accept every poem sent to them providing you buy the anthology. However, at the time I thought it was amazing and I could not believe my poem was actually in a book, it was so exciting. I bought two copies and still have them in my bookcase, to remind me of my poetry journey.

What publication are you most proud to have your work published in, why?

The poetry collection I am most proud of is my haiku seasons collection exploring the changes the Devon countryside undergoes with the change of each season. Haiku Yellow for spring, the upcoming Haiku Sun, Haiku Gold for autumn, and Haiku Ice, my winter collection. It has taken me five years to finish the collection and I consider it to be my poetic symphony. The Haiku collection has spread the word of haiku to many different countries and been accepted into haiku collections which is a huge honour and something I never expected.

Do you have a favourite genre of poetry?

My favourite genre of poetry is haiku, of course! However, I love the Romantic Poets and anything that makes me laugh or think or appreciate a beautiful descriptive narrative. The poems that have been significant to me are:

'She Walks in Beauty' by Lord Byron

'If' by Rudyard Kipling

'Stop all the clocks, cut off the telephone' by W. H. Auden

'Sea Fever' by John Masefield

Do you have a favourite writing space?

My favourite writing spaces are either my desk or in the quiet corner of a noisy café.

What projects are you working on and why?

My plans as a writer are huge!

This year the final book in my haiku seasons collection, 'Haiku Sun' is going to be published. I am working on my high fantasy novel, 'Resurgence' which will be published in 2021. At the same time, I am writing the prequel to my paranormal detective series, the first book in the series, 'Welcome To Witherleigh' which was published last year.

HAIKU NATION

www.ingramcontent.com/pod-product-compliance
Lightning Source LLC
Chambersburg PA
CBHW040107120526
44589CB00039B/2772